TAKE ACTION WITH ANIMALS!

ANIMALS IN THE SNOW

Written by
Madeline Tyler

Illustrated by
Amy Li

WINDMILL BOOKS

Published in 2022 by Windmill Books,
an Imprint of Rosen Publishing
29 East 21st Street, New York, NY 10010

This edition is published by arrangement with Booklife Publishing

Edited by: John Wood
Illustrated by: Amy Li

Cataloging-in-Publication Data

Names: Tyler, Madeline. | Li, Amy.
Title: Animals in the snow / by Madeline Tyler, illustrated by Amy Li.
Description: New York : Windmill Books, 2022. | Series: Take action with animals!
Identifiers: ISBN 9781499487428 (pbk.) | ISBN 9781499487442 (library bound) | ISBN 9781499487435 (6 pack) | ISBN 9781499487459 (ebook)
Subjects: LCSH: Animals--Polar regions--Juvenile fiction. | Tundra animals--Juvenile fiction.
Classification: LCC PZ7.1.T954 An 2022 | DDC [E]--dc23

Printed in the United States of America

CPSIA Compliance Information: Batch CSWM22: For Further Information contact Rosen Publishing, New York, New York at 1-800-237-9932

All images courtesy of Shutterstock. With thanks to Getty Images, Thinkstock Photo, and iStockphoto.

Cover - KateChe, Pattern image, flovie, Toluk, Anna Timoshenko, masher. Recurring backgrounds and font - KateChe, Pattern image, malven57. Recurring brushes - Toluk (grunge), flovie (spots/snow), Anna Timoshenko (rock cracks), Grinbox (animal fur), Irina Vaneeva, ekmelica (water splashes), Igor Vitkovskiy (snow flakes). 4-7 – masher, Nadezhda Molkentin, 22-23 – oxanakot, Tartila.

Can you use your imagination to take a trip through the snow?

Follow the

INSTRUCTIONS

on each page and see what you can find.

This **polar bear**
is covered in snow!

Can you

SHAKE

this book and then turn the page?

That is much better!

These **penguins** are walking in a line.

POKE

the penguins gently
and then turn the page.

Oops, the penguins
have slipped on the ice!

There is an **orca**
swimming in the sea.

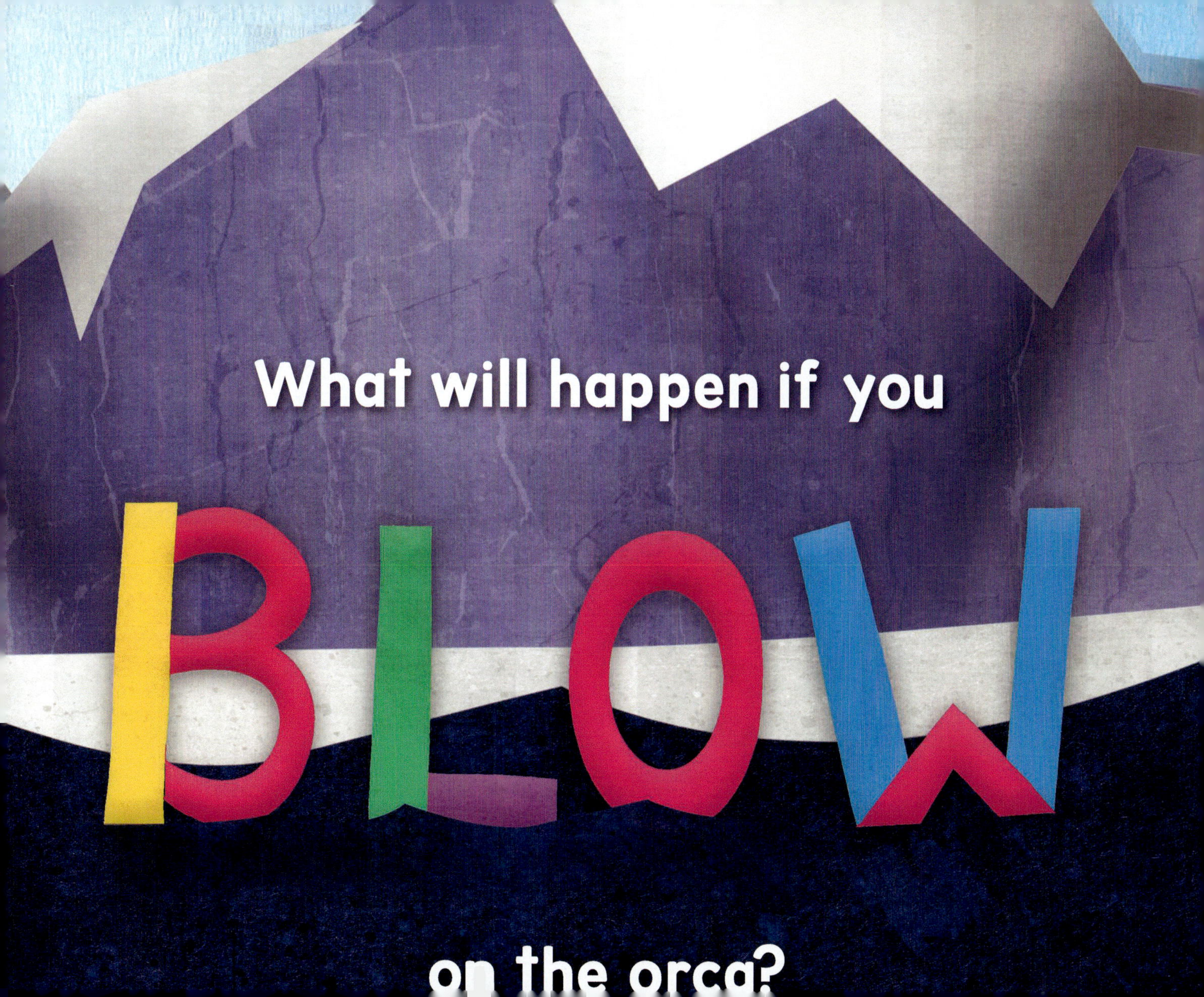

What will happen if you

BLOW

on the orca?

The orca is blowing through its blowhole!

That is how it breathes.

There are some **seals** on this iceberg.

Can you

TIP

this book to the left and turn the page?

That looks like fun!

Who is hiding under the water?

HOLD YOUR BREATH

and turn the page. Are you ready?

It is a **narwhal!**

Look at that long tooth!

Can you count all the animals in the picture?